# Airplanes and Balloons

## Words by Howard W. Kanetzke

Juvenile Publications Editor
State Historical Society of Wisconsin

Raintree Childrens Books
Milwaukee • Toronto • Melbourne • London

Library of Congress Number: 77-27532

5   6   7   8   9   0   82   81

Printed and bound in the United States of America.

Library of Congress Cataloging in Publication Data

Kanetzke, Howard W.
    Airplanes and balloons.

    (Read about)
    Bibliography: p.
    Includes index.
    SUMMARY:  An introduction to the history of
airplanes and balloons with a description of
different types and how they work.
    1.  Airplanes—Juvenile literature.  2.  Balloons
—Juvenile literature.  [1.  Airplanes.
2.  Balloons]  I.  Title.
TL547.M68      629.133      77-27532
ISBN 0-8393-0090-5 lib. bdg.

# Airplanes and
# Balloons

People have always wanted to fly. They watched birds in the sky. Then they made copies of birds' wings. They flapped these wings with their arms and tried to fly. But they could not stay in the air.

People finally got into the sky. They used big balloons. They knew that hot air rises. So they filled balloons with hot air. The balloons rose up into the sky.

**Montgolfier balloon
1783**

Some balloons
were filled with gas.
Gas is lighter than
air. So gas balloons
rose higher than hot
air balloons.

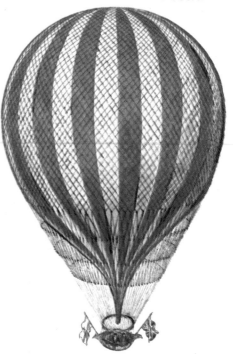

**Grand balloon
of Nassau**

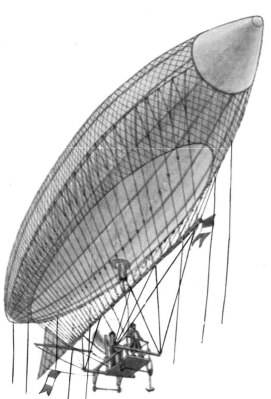

Other balloons
were driven by
engines. They could
be steered. Such
balloons were called
airships.

**Giffard's airship
1852**

Balloons once helped French soldiers. In 1870, Paris was surrounded by enemy soldiers. Balloons carried messages to French soldiers outside the city.

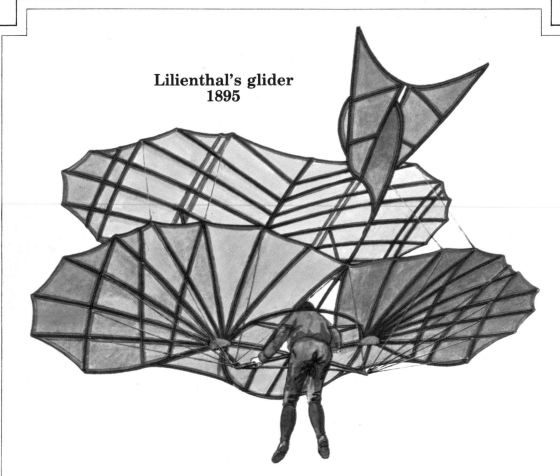

**Lilienthal's glider
1895**

Some people still tried to fly with wings. However, they no longer flapped the wings. Instead, they kept the wings still and floated like a kite. This is called gliding.

**Wright brothers'**
*Flyer I*
**1903**

In 1903, two Americans built an airplane with an engine. Their names were Orville and Wilbur Wright. Their airplane was the first to fly under its own power. Balloons flew because they were lighter than air. Airplanes were heavier than air. Yet these men had found a way to make them fly.

**airfoil**

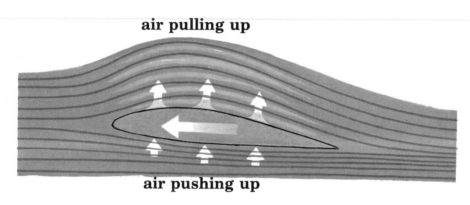

**air pulling up**

**air pushing up**

Airplane wings have a special shape.
They are called airfoils. As the plane moves
forward, each airfoil, or wing, pushes
through the air. The air flowing over the
wing curls around the top curve. The
distance over the wing from front to back is
greater than the distance under it. So the
air over the wing must move faster than
the air underneath. The slower air
underneath pushes up on the wing.

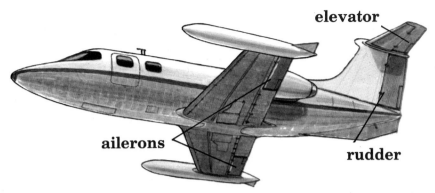

elevator

ailerons

rudder

Today there are moving parts on airplane wings and tails. They make the airplane change direction. The moving parts on the tail are called elevators. They help the plane go up or down. The ailerons on the wings make the plane tilt to one side. Then the rudder makes the tilted plane turn.

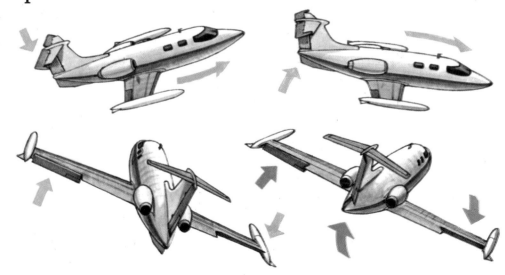

**Santos-Dumont's 14-bis
1906**

In the early 1900s, many people began making airplanes. Each builder tried to make a faster plane. This plane was built by a Frenchman. His name was Santos-Dumont. His was the first European plane to fly under its own power. It was called a biplane because it had two sets of wings.

Roe's triplane was one of the first English planes. The Voisin biplane was the first practical European plane. The Farman, however, was easier to fly than the Voisin.

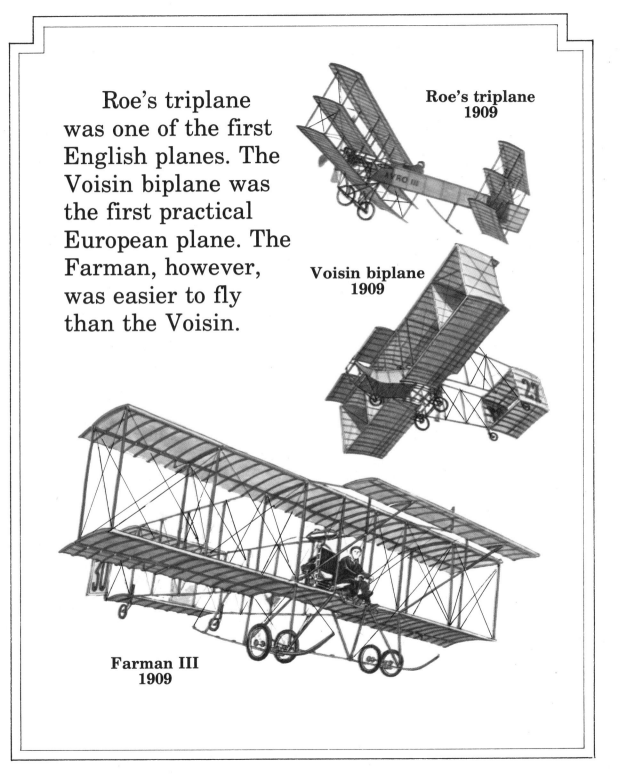

Roe's triplane
1909

Voisin biplane
1909

Farman III
1909

Early airplanes could stay in the air only a short time. It was dangerous to fly them over water. But Blériot, a Frenchman, knew he had a good airplane. He flew it safely across the English Channel from France to England.

**Blériot's XI monoplane
1909**

By 1909 airships were flying long distances from country to country. Passengers got onto this airship from a lake. The cabins were under the airship. Airships were popular for many years.

**Zeppelin airship
1910**

F.E.2B
1915

Fokker E.III
Eindecker

Airplanes became important in World War I. Many new styles of planes were developed. This Fokker airplane had a special gun. The bullets were fired through the moving propeller. But the bullets were set not to hit the moving blades.

Some airplanes dropped bombs. Other planes were used to watch the enemy from above. Pilots found many new uses for airplanes.

**S.E.5A
1918**

There were many airplanes left after the war. So people began to travel by airplane. Airplanes called airliners were built to hold passengers.

**Fokker F.VIIa-3m
1925
(3m means 3 motors)**

**D.H.60 Moth**

Some of the planes left from World War I were too small to carry many passengers. People flew them for sport. Pilots started flying clubs. Members bought small airplanes like this one.

Douglas DC-3
1935

Builders began to make airplanes out of
light metal. The landing wheels of new
planes could be raised while flying.

Igor Sikorsky developed a new kind of flying machine. It is called a helicopter. Airplanes have propellers in front of the engines. Helicopters, however, have big propellers on top. People had tried to make helicopters for years. Sikorsky was the first to make the idea work.

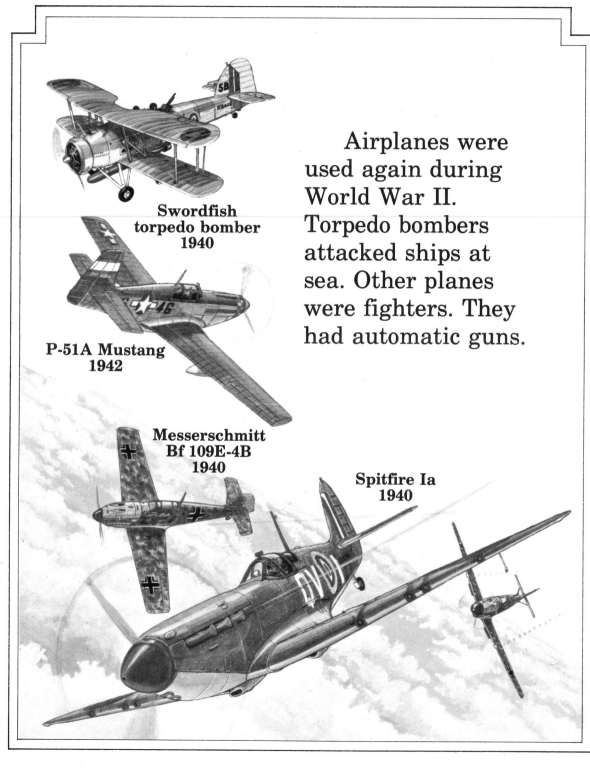

Swordfish
torpedo bomber
1940

P-51A Mustang
1942

Messerschmitt
Bf 109E-4B
1940

Spitfire Ia
1940

Airplanes were used again during World War II. Torpedo bombers attacked ships at sea. Other planes were fighters. They had automatic guns.

Heavy bombers were another kind of warplane. They had special places to hold bombs. A few bombs could be dropped at a time.

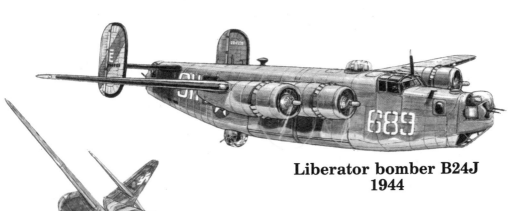

Liberator bomber B24J
1944

Me 262A-1A
1945

Jet fighters, like this one, were built near the end of World War II.

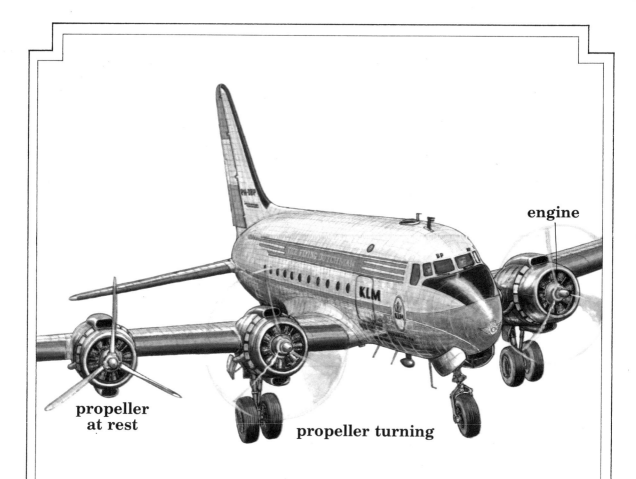

engine

propeller
at rest

propeller turning

Before World War II, all airplanes had
propellers. Engines made the propellers
turn. Propeller blades have a special shape.
They cut through the air. This action pulls
an airplane forward.

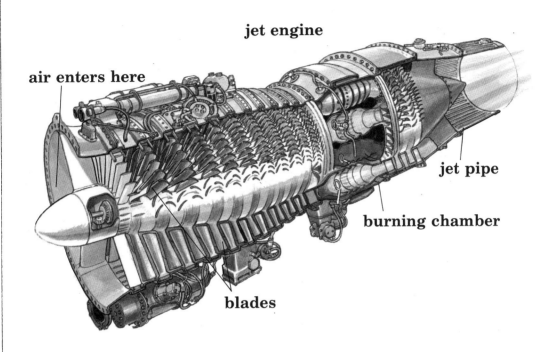

jet engine

air enters here

jet pipe

burning chamber

blades

The first planes to have jet engines were used in World War II. Jet engines pull in air at the front. Small blades push the air into a chamber. Inside, it is mixed with a fine spray of fuel. When this mixture is burned, it explodes. Then the exploding gases shoot out of the jet pipe. They push the plane forward.

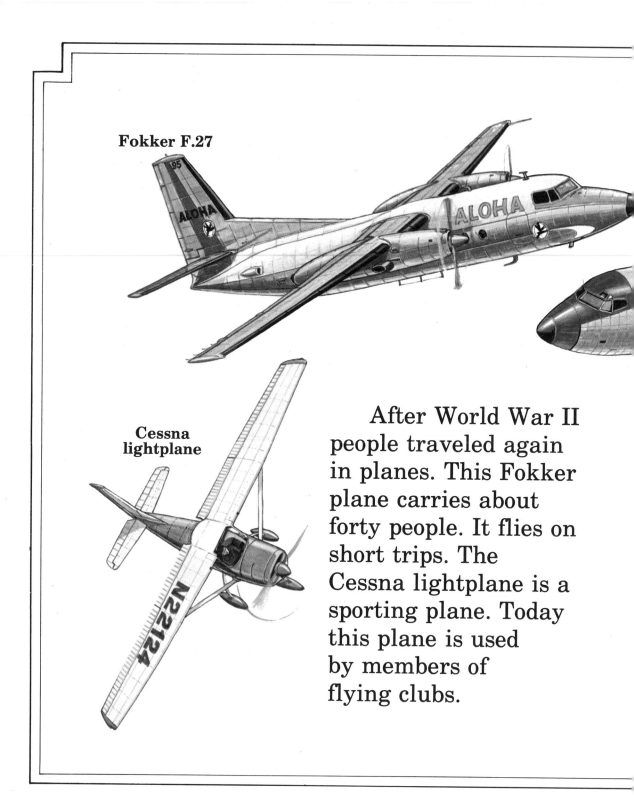

**Fokker F.27**

**Cessna lightplane**

After World War II people traveled again in planes. This Fokker plane carries about forty people. It flies on short trips. The Cessna lightplane is a sporting plane. Today this plane is used by members of flying clubs.

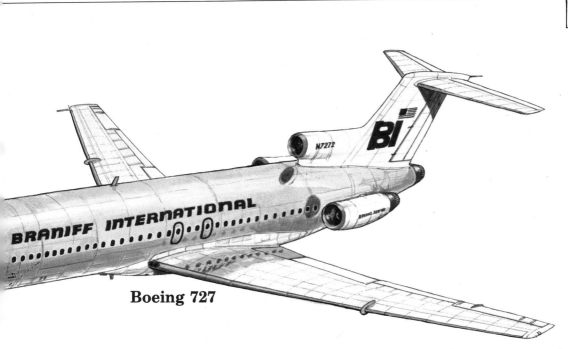

**Boeing 727**

Jet engines can power large airplanes. Jets fly farther than airplanes with propellers. Passenger jets were made bigger and bigger. This Boeing has seats for about 100 people.

**MiG-15
Russian**

Here are two jet warplanes. The
Russian plane is a jet fighter. The
American plane was built to do
several jobs.

**McDonnell Douglas
Phantom F-4B
1965**

**Hawker Siddeley
Harrier GR Mk 1**

This plane is called a VTOL. The letters stand for "vertical takeoff and landing." Most planes must go down a runway to take off. They do this to build up enough speed to fly. The VTOL rises straight up into the air.

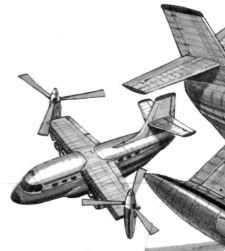

Designers are still working to make airplanes that fly faster and work better. They have designed a swing-wing bomber. Its wings fold back when it is flying. This gives the plane a smoother shape. It helps the plane to go fast.

two positions
of wing

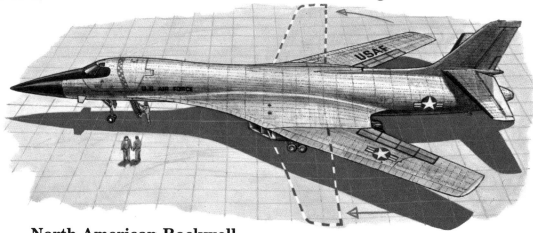

**North American Rockwell
B-1 bomber**

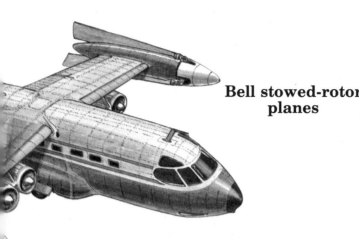

**Bell stowed-rotor planes**

A stowed-rotor airplane takes off straight up like a helicopter. The special propellers fold away when the plane is in the air. Then it flies like other planes.

This airplane is called a QSTOL. This means "quiet short takeoff and landing." It will be quieter than planes we use today.

**BAC QSTOL airliner**

**B-29 Superfortress**

**Bell X-1
1947**

Designers try to build faster airplanes. Pilots try to break speed records with new planes. This Bell X-1 plane was the first to fly faster than sound. It flew at nearly 1,000 miles per hour (1,600 kilometers per hour). It was carried into the air and let go by the other plane.

Airplanes that fly faster than sound are called supersonic. The Concorde is a supersonic airliner. It flies at twice the speed of sound.

**North American
X-15A**

The American X-15A has flown at more than 4,000 miles per hour (6,400 kilometers per hour).

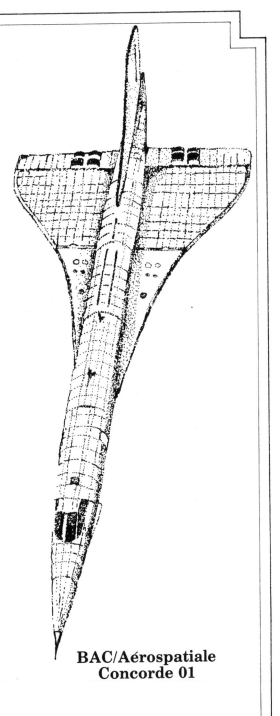

**BAC/Aérospatiale
Concorde 01**

# The Metric System

In the United States, things are measured in inches, pounds, quarts, and so on. Most countries of the world use centimeters, kilograms, and liters for these things. The United States uses the American system to measure things. Most other countries use the metric system. By 1985, the United States will be using the metric system, too.

In some books, you will see two systems of measurement. For example, you might see a sentence like this: "That bicycle wheel is 27 inches (69 centimeters) across." When all countries have changed to the metric system, inches will not be used any more. But until then, you may sometimes have to change measurements from one system to the other. The chart on the next page will help you.

All you have to do is multiply the unit of measurement in Column 1 by the number in Column 2. That gives you the unit in Column 3.

Suppose you want to change 5 inches to centimeters. First, find inches in Column 1. Next, multiply 5 times 2.54. You get 12.7. So, 5 inches is 12.7 centimeters.

| Column 1 | Column 2 | Column 3 |
|---|---|---|
| THIS UNIT OF MEASUREMENT | TIMES THIS NUMBER | GIVES THIS UNIT OF MEASUREMENT |
| inches | 2.54 | centimeters |
| feet | 30. | centimeters |
| feet | .3 | meters |
| yards | .9 | meters |
| miles | 1.6 | kilometers |
| ounces | 28. | grams |
| pounds | .45 | kilograms |
| fluid ounces | .03 | liters |
| pints | .47 | liters |
| quarts | .95 | liters |
| gallons | 3.8 | liters |
| | | |
| centimeters | .4 | inches |
| meters | 1.1 | yards |
| kilometers | .6 | miles |
| grams | .035 | ounces |
| kilograms | 2.2 | pounds |
| liters | 33.8 | fluid ounces |
| liters | 2.1 | pints |
| liters | 1.06 | quarts |
| liters | .26 | gallons |

# Where to Read About
# Airplanes and Balloons

# Pronunciation Key

| | |
|---|---|
| a | a as in **cat, bad** |
| ā | a as in **able**, ai as in **train**, ay as in **play** |
| ä | a as in **father, car**, o as in **cot** |
| e | e as in **bend, yet** |
| ē | e as in **me**, ee as in **feel**, ea as in **beat**, ie as in **piece**, y as in **heavy** |
| i | i as in **in, pig**, e as in **pocket** |
| ī | i as in **ice, time**, ie as in **tie**, y as in **my** |
| o | o as in **top**, a as in **watch** |
| ō | o as in **old**, oa as in **goat**, ow as in **slow**, oe as in **toe** |
| ô | o as in **cloth**, au as in **caught**, aw as in **paw**, a as in **all** |
| oo | oo as in **good**, u as in **put** |
| ō̄o | oo as in **tool**, ue as in **blue** |
| oi | oi as in **oil**, oy as in **toy** |
| ou | ou as in **out**, ow as in **plow** |
| u | u as in **up, gun**, o as in **other** |
| ur | ur as in **fur**, er as in **person**, ir as in **bird**, or as in **work** |
| yo͞o | u as in **use**, ew as in **few** |
| ə | a as in **again**, e as in **broken**, i as in **pencil**, o as in **attention**, u as in **surprise** |
| ch | ch as in **such** |
| ng | ng as in **sing** |
| sh | sh as in **shell, wish** |
| th | th as in **three, bath** |
| th̲ | th as in **that, together** |

# GLOSSARY

These words are defined the way they are used in this book

**aileron** (ā′ lə rän′) a moving part of an airplane's wing that tilts the plane to one side

**airfoil** (er′ foil′) a curved object that moves in a certain way through the air

**airliner** (er′ lī′ nər) a large airplane that carries passengers

**airship** (er′ ship′) an aircraft that is lighter than air and can be steered

**attack** (ə tak′) to start to fight against

**automatic** (ô tə mat′ ik) working by itself; without outside control

**biplane** (bī′ plān′) an airplane with two sets of wings

**blade** (blād) one of many long, narrow pieces of metal on a propeller

**bomb** (bom) an object that explodes

**bullet** (bool′ it) a small metal object that is shot out of a gun

**chamber** (chām′ bər)  an enclosed space

**club** (klub)  a group of people who meet and have the same interests

**designer** (di zīn′ ər)  a person who plans how a thing should be made

**develop** (di vel′ əp)  to come or bring into being

**elevator** (el′ ə vā′ tər)  a moving part on the tail of a plane, which helps the plane to go up or down

**engine** (en′ jin)  a machine that uses energy to run other machines

**explode** (eks plōd′)  to burst out suddenly from a confined space

**finally** (fin′ əl ē)  at last; at the end of a long time

**flap** (flap)  to move up and down in the air

**float** (flōt)  to move slowly above the ground

**fold** (fōld)  for one part of a thing to bend over and lie flat against another

**fuel** (fyōo′ əl)  a substance that is burned
  to provide energy

**gas** (gas)  a substance, like air, that is
  not solid or liquid

**glide** (glīd)  to fly without a motor

**helicopter** (hel′ ə kop′ tər)  an aircraft
  that flies by means of a large propeller
  on top

**jet** (jet)  an airplane driven by a stream
  of hot gas

**kilometers per hour** (ki lom′ ə terz
  pur our′)  a speed measured by the
  number of kilometers something travels
  in one hour

**kite** (kīt)  a light wooden frame, usually
  covered with paper, that is flown in the
  wind at the end of a string

**manage** (man′ ij)  to be able to do something

**member** (mem′ bər)  someone who
  belongs to a group

**message** (mes′ ij)  information carried
  from one person to another

**metal** (met′ əl) a substance that is usually hard and has a shiny surface, used to make many objects and machines

**miles per hour** (mīlz′ pur our′) a speed that is measured by the number of miles something travels in one hour

**mix** (miks) to put different things together

**mixture** (miks′ chər) a substance made of different things put together

**passenger** (pas′ ən jər) a person who is taken from one place to another in a vehicle

**pilot** (pī′ lət) a person who operates an aircraft

**pipe** (pīp) a tube which carries gases or liquids

**popular** (pop′ yə lər) liked by many people

**power** (pou′ ər) the energy which allows something to work

**practical** (prak′ ti kəl) working well and sensibly

**propeller** (prə pel′ ər) the part of a plane or boat that is made of long blades that turn around and around on a hub

**raise** (rāz) to cause something to move up

**record** (rek′ ərd) a performance that is better than any other

**rise** (rīz) to move upward

**rudder** (rud′ ər) a movable part on the tail of an aircraft that helps it to turn

**runway** (run′ wā) a long, narrow place where planes take off and land

**set** (set) a group of things that are alike in some way

**speed** (spēd) a rate of motion; quick or fast motion

**sport** (spôrt) something that is done for fun

**spray** (sprā) a group of tiny drops of a liquid

**steer** (stēr) to guide the movement of something

**stowed-rotor airplane** (stōd′ rōt ər
er′ plān) an airplane that has
propellers that fold back by the engines
after the plane takes off

**style** (stīl) a particular kind of design or
way of building something

**supersonic** (sōō′ pər sän′ ik) past the
speed of sound

**surround** (sə round′) to be all around

**swing-wing bomber** (swing′ wing
bom′ ər) an airplane that has wings
that fold back along its body

**takeoff** (tāk′ ôf) the motion of rising up
into flight

**tilt** (tilt) to raise one side

**torpedo** (tôr pē′ dō) a long metal shell
that moves underwater and explodes
when it hits something

**travel** (trav′ əl) to move from one place
to another

**triplane** (trī′ plān′) a plane that has
three sets of wings

**vertical** (vur′ ti kəl) moving straight up
and down

**warplane** (wôr′ plān) a plane used in
fighting wars

# Bibliography

Allward, Maurice. *All Kinds of Airplanes.* New York:
Grosset and Dunlap, Inc., 1971.

Everds, John. *It Began with Jenny: A History of
Air Transportation.* Chicago: Rand McNally and
Co., 1972.

Kelly, James E., and Park, William R. *The Airport Builders.*
Reading, Mass.: Addison-Wesley Publishing Co., 1973.

Morgan, Julie. *Airplane.* Philadelphia: J. B.
Lippincott Co., 1972.

Ross, Frank, Jr. *Flying Paper Airplane Models.*
New York: Lothrop, Lee and Shepard Co., 1975.

Sotomayor, Antonio. *Balloons: The First Two
Hundred Years.* New York: G. P. Putnam's
Sons, 1972.

Urquhart, David Inglis. *The Airplane and How
It Works.* New York: Henry Z. Walck, Inc., 1973.

Williams, Brian. *Aircraft.* New York: Warwick
Press, 1974.